Kitchen Heat

KITCHEN HEAT

— POEMS —

Ava Leavell Haymon

To Peter & Ann —
for our many years of
friendship and shared
experience —
Love

LOUISIANA STATE UNIVERSITY PRESS
BATON ROUGE

Ava Leavell Haymon

Published by Louisiana State University Press
Copyright © 2006 by Ava Leavell Haymon
All rights reserved
Manufactured in the United States of America
First printing

Designer: Barbara Neely Bourgoyne
Typeface: Whitman, text; Trajan Pro, display
Typesetter: G & S Typesetters, Inc.
Printer and binder: Edwards Brothers, Inc.

Library of Congress Cataloging-in-Publication Data
Haymon, Ava Leavell.
  Kitchen heat : poems / Ava Leavell Haymon.
    p. cm.
  ISBN-13: 978-0-8071-3171-8 (alk. paper)
  ISBN-10: 0-8071-3171-7 (alk. paper)
  ISBN-13: 978-0-8071-3172-5 (pbk. : alk. paper)
  ISBN-10: 0-8071-3172-5 (pbk. : alk. paper)
I. Title.
PS3608.A945K58 2006
811'.6—dc22

2005031103

NATIONAL
ENDOWMENT
FOR THE ARTS

This publication is supported in part by an award from
the National Endowment for the Arts.

The paper in this book meets the guidelines for permanence and durability
of the Committee on Production Guidelines for Book Longevity
of the Council on Library Resources. ∞

To my grandmother

Ava Carroll Watkins Collier David

Contents

BABIES' BONES FROM MAGIC CRYSTALS

KITCHEN HEAT

What the Magnolias Say

The postcard azaleas are over. All lavender racemes
a month ago, wisteria's gone to bumptious vine.
Pastel can't bear the heat. Winsome printemps
fragrances go north with prissy finches.
The high for the day exceeds the melting point
of light wax, and spring in Baton Rouge slumps over

into summer. The hot days
stun themselves silly with spores and dampness.
The first week in May. All the flowers are white—
ligustrum, sweet olive, jasmine up against the chain link.
Bruised gardenias ooze a coded ester, and padlocked
doors sag backwards to the Cretaceous past:
sticky and narcotic, the magnolias heave open
heaviest, whitest of all.

Harem incense streams off creamy petals,
the tarry background odor of family sins
visited on children, of flesh sins hidden
in the linens, laced with vetiver against mildew—
dizzy whiff of hand-ripped cypress, slave-rigged
into room after room, a house bedded on dust
from a thousand overflows. The sweetish smell
of survival by any means.

It's old as sharks, this tough old plant.
Holdout from the first mother Angiosperm
who crossed seduction and pollen, made herself
a true seed, all wrapped up in itself, and bound
to change the rules of history: Moses, floated
by his sister into simple Nile bulrushes.

Flicker in the light: a woman's face recoils
across the whorl of petals—left to right—vellum

paging back to the beginning. The drowsy calyx
swells to fruit on the tree of knowledge.
Reach out your hand, hums the unctuous air,
potent as lithium. *Take them both, male/female,
the split halves of my dicot heart.*

CHOOSING MONOGAMY

Hunting and Gathering

There's leftover venison in the house. All sliced,
a fine gray-brown, pink at the center, no fat.
Packed in Ziploc gallon bags in a dark roux gravy
from the pan drippings and lots of cracked pepper.
It's dead meat, as the kids say to mean something's
about to be destroyed. The tense confuses present/future
as the two of us have, making a boy and a girl child.

You shot this buck, or the boy did, or maybe it's a doe.
I always roast the haunches with garlic. There's too much,
more than we'll ever eat. The refrigerator won't close,
the freezer grumbles through the night. We chew
and chew, swallow hard—heat it up in pans
of all sizes, try to think of different vegetables.
Our steak knives saw back and forth, our stomachs,
our teeth begin to feel middle-aged, and still
the bullet moves in through the shoulder and stops
          the bewildered heart.

Endangered Habitat

I bring a rhinoceros with me,
dusty, implacable as the broad veldt, the great horn
an aphrodisiac. Its source of value

the very cause of its extinction. The horn
is made of hair, I've read, a crowning glory.
I bring a rhinoceros with me,

a raw beauty that won't be owned.
It shoulders through glass walls, the owner's castle,
an aphrodisiac, a source of value.

Cocktails follow committees, I dress the part,
keep my voice down. I'm small and southern,
bring a rhinoceros with me.

Two eldest children, both grown out of danger,
contract this marriage. I violate the terms.
The aphrodisiac, a source of value

in other quarters, swells the cells with fear first.
Our bond: once endangered, twice shy. I change
the rules. I bring a rhinoceros with me:
aphrodisiac, source, value.

Bandera Roja

after André Breton

My husband whose hair is spices
Whose chest is beagles and chicory
Whose chest is alive with climbing vines and thickets of owls
My husband whose shoulders are old ivory, are a burning tower,
      are fire at the windows, are the sand floor of a bay
My husband whose throat is anger, is red stars, is forced singing
Whose throat is galls of the black oak
My husband whose back is a wood boat whose timbers ease the wind
The trunk of the coco palm in the wind
Whose back shines like onyx and steel alloy
Whose forehead is a round marble, hard and valuable
Whose eyes are questions and questions
Whose eyes are the throwing of dice
      and the yellow light of the gaming table
Whose ears, a bird before feathers
Whose lips are all of Mexico
My husband whose lips are a hurricane
Whose lips are a hurricane bearing up the river channel
Whose lips bear up the river's course from the Gulf
Whose lips bear danger and moisture and the saltbreath of the sea
Whose voice speaks in the night the turning stars
Whose voice is the current of the warm river
My husband whose voice is the first news of storm
Whose arms are sycamores in heavy wind
Whose arms are the brittle-limbed white trees in spring squalls
Whose arms are the leap of fish in the Gulf
      and the horizon lost in a damp haze

Rare Night Out

. . . one of those movies where everything's unrelated so you
think there's a MEANING
—overheard in a ticket line at the Broadmoor Theater

On the screen in a darkened movie house, my own breasts
glowed back at me from a dressing-room mirror,
my everyday dress transparent as a lens.
The lunging bluefish ran with my line. My exposed liver
throbbed with a masterful presence that merged
with the whirring from the projection room
and palled the hospital scene to insignificance.

Where from here do I go, now that the mask is off
the surgeon? Do I dangle by ropes tied to my ankles
and make chalk rubbings of the masonry of the skyscraper?
Am I, rubbing away at the red bricks high above the street,
myself the fish on a hook from someone else's boat?
Is what happens in front of us a hieroglyph for treasure
maps, a plan of salvation, old family recipes?

If the film drive in the projector locks,
will we stare slack-faced at one frame?
our children's round faces, say?
while it melts from the unwavering attention
and runs down into sprocketed gears
and we are knocked blind by the unbordered,
uncolored, unflickering light?

All the Men in My Family Hunt

I don't hear the alarm. Usually
I don't even wake up when you leave.
You drive up together to George's land
in the Felicianas, to hunt wild turkey.
Thermos, coffee breath, jokes in the truck.
Jokes women wouldn't laugh at, jokes
about too much bourbon, the girl
who couldn't get enough. I move over
into the warm spot on your side.

George told me you have to be in the woods
a full hour before first light, someplace
you've seen the birds before, and there
you make the sound of an owl.
Turkeys hate owls so much, they stir
on their roosts and grumble in their sleep.
My mother once told me Daddy heard an owl
the night before he died. I asked her later
what kind of owl it is you hear before you die.
She said, the owl who knows your name.

Anyway, George says you listen for that hoarse gobble
and haul ass toward it, shotgun vertical
in front of you so the stickers won't cut your face.
You can't see. You try to get yourself
into range the exact moment of gray dawn.
If you're early, you'll run up too close, and
they'll hear you before you can see to take aim.
If you're late, they see you coming and fly off
before you're close enough to shoot.

The window by the bed begins to show its frame.
I remember daylight, maybe afternoon.
I'm nine or ten, I walk behind his slumping bulk
for miles, carrying the shotgun. Bisque-colored road ruts

fill with sweetgum leaves, with sycamore sticks,
the cold gun barrel bumps its bruise of honor
against my skinny collarbone. At some signal
I do not hear, he lightens, turns like a dancer
and takes the gun, whispers, *Be quiet.*
Later—I'd stood at attention for half an hour—
he comes back uphill, shakes his head, which is all
the story I expect, and there the memory leaves off.

I know what wild turkey looks like
only from the whiskey bottle, but I ate it once
at your mother's—firm, deep brown meat,
even the breast. It was Thanksgiving,
we were grateful. A dense earth taste
like gun smoke, black walnuts, tar.
In the pillows and the empty bed,
I'm rousing with the urge to kill and eat.
I was 22 years old and we'd just got married.
All the men in my family hunt. Jokes
women wouldn't laugh at *anymore*, I mean:
back then I used to laugh at them during dinner.
Under the covers, I move my legs to find the place
you left, and half-dream you and George

waiting under sable trees, when you can't see
each other's features or even uprightness,
imitating animal calls you practiced driving up.
Listening for the grumpy sounds of sleep,
running full tilt in the slap dark, guns loaded,
falling across streambeds, armadillo holes, crashing
through blackberries and sticker vines you'd duck under
any other time. Chasing—we are all chasing,
the dream is ending—chasing the shy wild bird I tasted
only that once, I still remember it in my mouth.
Trying to be the owl who knows its name.

Winter Migration Patterns

From the glass porch, where the rhinoceros
spent a humid December, human female watches
mate drag Christmas tree across wet yard
and down toward street. Every few steps
the male glares at another scratch pit in the lawn.
Armadillos, this far north now. Both mates think

something must be done.
Male juts his head out ahead of his shoulders
like a yoked water buffalo. Bovine,
his mouth hangs open, an adenoidal sag
that signals female he is angry, resents
the task, is imposed upon, disappointed

in the holiday, her flawed gift to him.
Out of habit, she morphs back into rhinoceros,
casts tiny single-purpose eye down plated shoulder.
Her vigilance has waned, however. The holiday's
over; she can afford to be human again.
Female is grateful the shedding tree is gone

but exasperated at herself. Needing his help
has roused her primate shame at being
the weaker of the species: this affect emerges
as cuteness is outgrown. *Christmas Eve
midnight, the dumb beasts speak,* female repeated
during the last weeks, several times.

Her mate is tired of her little sayings. Not mallards,
not swans, these are land creatures unsuited
for lifetime monogamy. Successful cohabitation
would be project enough. This holiday season, the first
without a child in the house, the oldest fears
are never far. Female hides, calculates escape routes.

In her mate's breathing she hears
constriction, the mulish rage of abandonment,
the injured young simian who tries to earn status
or at least protection from the adult females
of his group. Tries good behavior. Tries silence.
Neither is successful. He tries harder.

What signs does male respond to here?
He will not say, does not make images.
Plod, plod, hauls the tree behind him
like a plow. Like mute beasts
in ordinary time, their moment of speech
past, these two monitor each other's bodies:

jawbones, pupils, goose bumps,
snorts or slowed breath, night smells.
The tree is to the curb. He leaves it there.
She stops watching. The animals,
wild and domesticated, fade back
into their separate habitats.

The year moves on. Songbirds
and mosquitoes will return
in time for spring.

Conjugal Love Poem

The day my husband said
I got this cold's been draggin on me
and I wanted to kick his teeth in—

Posture of the Victim, that's what
that's called. He'll say: How you doin this morning?

Great, I say (kinda spunky), How bout you?
His voice falls off a couple of notes:
      Oh, pretty good.
Or maybe I say, Oh pretty good, how about you?
      He says, Fair.

Or if I say fair,
      he says not so good

or if I say
not so good—how about you—you look terrible,
then he says,
      I got this cold's been draggin on me.

I'm thinking I'll catch something next to terminal.
He'd say
      How're you feelin this morning?
and I'd say
      Right at terminal, how about you?
and then
      he'd have to say   Dead.

Married, with Cancer

for Ruth and Stephen Vance

A former nun, her tongue buffs the Latin
to the pure vowels of a mezzo: *Medulla oblongata.*
It's the brain stem, she explains.
The main tumor was higher, in the cerebellum,
and they chopped that out. But it'd sent down
jellyfish legs into the brain stem. Skinny fingers
dangle a slow seaweed stir to demonstrate.
You can't operate on the medulla, so they radiated
to the maximum amount. Zot! zot! the fingers shoot
rays my direction, then curl to grip her raw
intention: *The brain stem's the seat of instinct.*
The soul. A fist. We've got to get it back.
Ruth collects case histories of psychic healing
the way the pious study lives of the saints—

I think of Saul on the road to Damascus,
struck blind and nameless by the great light.
My words are sharp cinders I cross barefoot:
Maybe you're asking too much. It's a confrontation
in her driveway. Ruth has walked me out to my car,
leaving Stephen in the curtained living room.
We squint in the noon glare. I press: *You want him*
to root out some deep personal flaw? Let him die!
I want to say. Too strenuous, too much clarity,
this cure, this change you demand. Her pupils tighten.
Blue-gray irises fold into the ridges of a dry feather.
I see myself made of tin, she answers. *A skeleton,*
with very few parts. Made to endure deep cold.
Flimsy latches hook my legs onto my backbone.

Inside the house, propped on a couch,
Stephen—who dreams nightly of boats—
spellbinds an audience of well-wishers.

He's arrayed in a cancer-ward costume, eye patch
of a pirate, hanks of hair in goofy islands,
telling stories from childhood: 1952,
a land rover trek from Nairobi,
the family arrives at the grand lobby
of the old Hotel Lake Mañara.
Mother and young sons, dusty and stiff
as camels, huddle close, scuttle through
and out of sight. Only when they are gone:
erect, impeccable, pride of the diplomatic corps,
the Father strolls in alone.

When the Father's post is Chad, the boys
are dispatched to the Swedish embassy
to learn the birds and bees from one Maurice,
who was known to be cautious and medical.
They are eleven and twelve. His advice,
in total, is this: *Want to make the Spanish girls
do handstands? Repeat after me:*
        "Bonita. Linda. Preciosa y guapa."
And in Fez on the flat roof of a four-tier mud house
—pigeon pie, lemon chicken stuffed with couscous,
mint, cucumbers in yogurt, chilled melon.
Served in slow courses with hashish, cinnamon.
The daughter of the house, breasts bare, breath
warm with cloves, pours rosewater for their hands.

The seared medulla smokes memory and ash,
a lifeflash before our eyes. In a dust cloud
of sandalwood the heady map of Stephen's
childhood uncurls on the living room floor,
corners escaping to scroll closed.
Childscript cartography fades rich
and sweet as Africa, as myrrh, as baklava.
Behind him, mute as a stage flat, a painting
on goatskin hangs on the wall. Stephen claims
he haggled it from a leper in Christian Ethiopia.

The burning of sheaves, Stephen explains.
Once a year only, when the rains come. Maskl,
he calls it, *the miracle of new flowers,* older
than the prophet Elijah who called down fire.

I back out to drive away, and Ruth, alone,
heads due north toward the darkening pole.
Out on the ice field she goes, shining
the dimestore flashlight of a fanatic. A tin woman,
no creature of temperature, she offers no flesh
to snag the elements. Under her metal prong feet,
a floe cracks away from the polar heart
along a seam blue and uneven as fate. It tips
side to side, the way a bateau nods underfoot
to buoy clear from the boat launch. She's lulled
by the motion, bound now in the cold sea journey
into the dark and the seasickness.
With nothing to carry it back home in,
she hunts down his future.

Prothalamion

for Sonja and Houston
after a painting by Meinrad Craighead

MARRIAGE: A PAINTING

In the foreground, a woman and man sleep
in a tumble of arms, legs, white sheets.
The night is dark, only a last bit of moon.
As they sleep, Time—a heavy serpent—slides
beside them along the ground. Its head and tail
extend beyond the edges of the canvas.
The Past is here, a mound of snake's eggs
in a little hollow scooped in the dirt. The eggs,
like the sheets, glow faintly in waning moonlight.

Sky and ground are a warm thick brown, the color,
in paintings as in dreams, that means night,
means the deep motions of the unconscious.
The Future, tall figure in a long red robe,
brings cascading armfuls of full-blown roses.
Her face is another moon, the promise of return
the waning moon always calls over its shoulder.

This man and woman, to sleep so deeply,
what disclosures have they made before
they slept? It is never easy, being this close,
and the world is dangerous. Daylight's
a clatter of voices—translation,
strategy, compromise, fact.

But here, in the brown night, only silence.
The woman and man sleep without needing
to dream. It is at last the Present,
and the trust that allows the animal self
to reinhabit the body, to breathe without censure,
to lay down the tools of forethought and language,
to inherit the old green earth. To do so together.

MARRIAGE: A CARTOON

You draw a kitchen table—piles of bills, applications,
yellow sticky notes, the last of some sandwiches.
On the wall, an angry calendar. A three-year-old
reaches up to pull the electrical cord of the coffee pot.

Where are the woman and man in this picture?
Do you sketch them in the next frame, serenely asleep
with a serpent on the ground in some fairy tale forest?
No. You put them here, in this kitchen. One standing,
hand on hip, grabbing the coffee pot just in time.

The other, hunched at the table over lists of numbers,
maybe holding a fussy baby, looks up in time to see
the split-second rescue of the coffee pot. And somehow—
out of all the possibilities—begins to laugh.

Where does it come from, this wellspring
of competence and stamina? the courage
to snatch time away from the calendar?
The moon is still there, looking through the window
over the sink, uninterested in the stacked dishes.
This is the only earth you inhabit, moon says
in its paper-white, unhurried way.

*This is the Present, this kitchen. Past and Future
reel about like unsprung clock hands.
It is never easy, being this close,
and the world is rather jealous.
Take up the tools of attention and language,
sharpen pencils. Draw this one moment.*

Quarrel: An Aftermath

At dawn, we met to fish
from the land bridge between
two lakes. My eyes were still
sleepy, but this is not a dream.

Three pelicans flew over us
low against a radiating sky.
Early morning light bored through
the outspread glide, and inside
the architecture of feathers

we saw the grotesque honesty
of scrawny blind bodies, a pitiful chest
and precious little below that,
yard-long wing bones
skinny as broken pencils.

An hour later, we've had our say
and the sun weighs impartially
on all heads. South of us, the lake shore
draws into an inlet, and the entire flock
has divided and settled—living together

the way we should all learn to do.
An outer formation thrashes wings
against water surface, to funnel fish in
toward the others, that float in a line
across the narrowing point of the vee.

Ordinary daylight: we see what we are
supposed to see—massive birds, archaic
and self-satisfied, gleaming like clean porcelain,
working the way they've always worked,
fishing for the same fish we are.

The Distance Between Us

Hwy 61, through the delta,
pay phone to call home.
Dialing—somebody waiting—
too many buttons, too many overnights
in different towns, couches
beside the bookcases
of strangers.

       Five rings, an answering
machine click, and my own voice recites
our number in the tone
of a mother shaming a child
in public. I want to be
in a book with you, our words
lying flat and calm on adjacent
pages, touching top to bottom
without changing the sentences at all,
not even a comma. I want the paperback
falling open by itself to that very page,
the book that leans sideways
in a gap on the shelf, sagging
a little in the spine.

Choosing Monogamy

I want to eat you whole and
I want to hold you like a baby.
I want to rub your hands
between mine. I want to rub
your back and legs with
cedar-smelling oils. I want to see
in your mouth. I want to pry up
under your eyelids. I want to watch
you pay bills and brush your teeth.

I want to be in Mexico with you.
I want your hand on my neck.
I want to be with you in a crowd
of village children. I want us to talk all night.
I want us to go to sleep early because we know
we have the next day. You hide something
from me that hurts you. I want you
to tell me what it is, where it is.
I want to put my hands on it.

I want to go with you to the beach.
I want us to watch the shorebirds together.
When the light falls and the gulls standing
in the shallows turn to face the wind change,
I want us to talk about monogamy,
and how wolves are that way, and sandpipers,
and how the only trouble with monogamy
is that it's not what we long for
and know we can never have.

Aphrodite

i

It's not just a cat dying
this time. It's Love
itself, impaled in this blind
arthritic flea-bite female,
whose last hold on her destiny
stares out green dinner-plate eyes
that do not blink. The cat has not blinked
in all her eighteen years.

Our last pet—it's come to this.
Love dribbles out, flesh
driven old and mad with it—
the boy gone off, the girl
grown—the dogs,
the other cats, countless fish,
the horned toad who died of a hug,
the ones that turned bottom up,
the ones that ran away, that ran
in front of cars, gerbils, a hamster,
a pair of ducks that never learned to fly
but waddled out of the yard (when
the steady vee of wings beating north
was seen in the sky) and into the mouth
of the neighbor's hound.

ii

We traveled together to the spring near Eleusis,
where Aphrodite bathed to renew her virginity
after every act of love. I splashed the cold water
on my neck, drizzled some down the front of my jeans
when no one was looking. The daughter back home
heard the stories from this place
her mother left her for,

and when kittens were born
—without father, without home,
without owner or welcome—
in the snaky damp crawl space
under the house, the dark
where no good child would ever go,
she named them Hermes, Hades, Aphrodite.

iii

Aphrodite, born without invitation,
a feral thing. The nameless mother chose
to set down her litter here, where we wanted
pedigrees, wanted to choose our pets,
abort the mistakes, spay the extras,
wanted to plan which animals to feed,
to care about, to pay the vet
outrageous fees for, none covered by insurance.

Hades ran away, after his mother,
and with her entered the realm of darkness,
and Hermes stayed, the favorite, quick and charming,
killer of squirrels, the messenger, and

Aphro, well, she was dumb and we made fun of her
and she followed her clever brother around
and looked confused, but she grew long hair,
soft and gray and white as doves' wings,
and was gloriously, pointlessly beautiful.
When she curled on the deck in the sun,
a background to frame her
would rush forward for the honor.

iv

She's still dumb and her geriatric cat food
costs fifteen dollars a sack, and this morning
she walked off the side of the porch
and fell in the aspidistra border.

We've had four mourning ceremonies
complete with songs, because we keep thinking
she's dying, and she will soon,
I'm convinced of it. While we sit

for breakfast at our small table
with only two plates and not much to talk about,
Aphrodite, the back yard behind her
a graveyard of other pets, pulls
her front feet under, wraps her balding tail
around them like it's a mantle of finest wool.
Turns her head toward us, locks her eyes
in our direction as though she could see,
and does not blink, and will not look away.

Envoi: Billy Doo

I want to write you about the bowl
so the bowl will be there, take shape
like coil clay stacking up
damp and heavy, one curl at a time.

I want the slip under my fingernails,
the pull of muddy water drying
on the backs of my hands.

Thumbs, pressing dents their own plump size,
the steam, later, rising from good soup.
You, hungry.

What Passes for Fall

We've rounded the equinox and turned toward
All Hallows when the paper finally promises
humidity below 50 percent. The high for the day
will simmer mosquitoes up from the ground,
but this morning's air takes on a burnished shine
and cleans itself like an orange cat.

It's never simple here: no sky signs visible
from my southeast window, only a flat chaos
of green. Pecan leaves, sweet gum, every shade
olive drab to March citrine, half already
spotted yellow and dropped. Like eyes
that watched all along, two squirrel's nests
show through now, near the crown.

My ghosts gather to me as they do
this time of year, to observe a liturgy
more formal than seasons in Baton Rouge.
They will stay until Candlemas.
Banish them, says more than one
mental health professional.
But I will be alone,

I answer as the eternal circle closes
into winter. One can count on the faithful beasts,
of course, but who else would stand
beside me then, at the fearsome manger
when the future is born
on the longest night of the year?

DEPENDABLE HEAT SOURCE

You Can See It in the Architecture

Gather 'round, Yankees—come out from inside
those masonry double walls and smallish windows, furnace
puffing away, an iron lung just under the carpet floor.
Southern houses are built in fear of heat.

Our haunts wear eyelet instead of sleeping caps
and shawls, and they tend to be young girls dead
of the yellow-fever afterbirth of a baby
that had to be strangled. Built of wood, inside and out,

high ceilings, a pine floor set on soft-brick piers,
footed in the flat boggy muck of overflows, raised
above swamp fire, mosquitoes. Roomy closets
stuffed with whatever it is we find to wrap bones in,

hung with bay laurel sprigs for the mildew. I'm describing
a tinderbox, you may have noticed, with bead-board wainscot
or floral wallpapers, and layer on layer of paint and wax.
They say you always become what you most fear.

With an attic. Always an attic. For the updraft,
don't you know? Old raw cypress smell there,
where the heat collects, builds, heat the downstairs
rooms were designed to hide, to funnel up here,

up here with the cobweb trunks that won't lock
anymore and the bundles of dry-rot doll clothes.
A dark triangle vault—listen close now, you'll be glad
you came outside—gluttonous for thermal increase,

hungry for a hundred oppressive summer afternoons,
till the hot red eye of memory flicks open
underneath its oily gauze bandages
and the whole structure is consumed.

White House in Watercolor

after a painting by Judi Betts

Late morning siennas bleed into cyanine green.
A two-story frame house carves itself
out of a mumble of shadows. Seven windows
sink back, double-sashed, vermilion, sulfur.
In the foreground, filed teeth dazzle
into fence pickets, their bases sheared off
in umbers uneven as wild onion and sourgrass.

Bare white paper glares under the north gable:
the shape, an archangel garment of bleached wool,
nothing to announce. An unpainted oval floats
on the porch wall, a jowled eyeless face.
And the front steps—more unmapped white,
edges erratic with camellia and bay laurel
and notched along one side with telltale right angles
to summon up the dirty boots of uncles.

This is not the idea of a house. Not the house
you could draw once your best friend
taught you the 3-D cube: a box to crawl into
from any side, a box that held nothing.
And it's not the Three Bears' tidy house
before the little sneak thief broke and entered,
broke some more and left blond corkscrew hairs
in the nap of the bedspread.

This is the house the light shines through,
where windows hold back secrets the shade
of fading bruises, and a cotton wad sags
on the screen door against haunts and mosquitoes.
The house where all the accidents happened
that left you the way you are—unable to face

a sheet of bare white paper till it's brushed over
with color you can't see through,
painted into uncertain shapes
you only claim to recognize.

Eye Games

In any bright room, the dark is there, waiting
to soak through at the first timid request.
I'll show you. For a moment

ignore the lively colors that reach toward
your face. Look straight at the charcoal
shadows even now trying to recede.
Take all the time you need. You'll see

the design relax, positive go negative.
The sables, the carbon blacks open
their hoarse throats, and the real dark
—the dark behind it all—eases in.

Try it again. See the sight plane as just that,
a two-dimension film before your eyes.
Rotate your head side to side, nod up/down.
Extrapolate. You'll find that the plane is small,

a pixel section of a hand-painted paper globe
that's no larger than a breakfast room
and you are inside it, sitting in a little highchair
at dead center, maybe a tray in front of you,

some red and yellow beads, or a nice spoon to bang.
All around you, the globe wraps tissue paper scenes,
mainly in pinks and blues, that rumple a bit
along the seams from the clumped paste.

Now focus on the small inked-in accents—
a man's black shoe here, the skinny hands
of a clock, one sliding behind the other, a daub
of burnt umber on the floor under the bookcase.

Look again. The ink disguises slits,
cigarette burns, failures in the delicate paper,
and here the humid dark pours through a syrup
of ashes, sticky as oil smoke, bitter with sulfur,

benzene, filling the globe, you in it still trapped
in that chair, the plastic belt cutting across
your soft stomach. You've dropped the spoon
and you've already learned nobody's coming

to pick it up for you. Your eyes fill
and you're no longer able to see
the pretty pictures, no longer able
even to believe they are there.

Heat

Butter, Crayolas, tar—edges wavered,
ran together—our mother's make-up,
chocolate, the ice blocks in sawdust.
My grandmother knew more
than one way to skin a cat.
She made me a chubby
baby chick out of yellow
modeling clay that lay
down, and in a single
July afternoon,
became an egg.

My grip goes
soft: I know the heat
hiding in the latitudes
waits to reduce us all
like the wax crèche figures
I unwrapped last Advent
season to find the Baby Jesus—
halo and all—melted into a headless
camel of the unlucky Wise Man, himself
dark and shapeless in the manger
with one of Mary's blue-white arms.

Old Grandmother Magic

My grandmother said
I could be a boy
when I kissed my elbow.

I skinned up into the old fig, hid
in the tropical smell of crushed mimosa,
warm baby's flesh, contorted myself
all afternoon. The green fruit swayed

and waved like weak-wristed southern beauties,
my shoulder sockets ached, the sweat
and prickle of failure, an itch
along my neck from the hairy leaves.

Too chicken to break my arm,
I yanked off all the swelling figs
I could reach and watched my little roost
streak slow with gluey milk sap.

Even now, I check to be sure:
my neck is stiffer,
I can't get my elbow
close to my mouth at all.

Sometimes when I'm sleepy
or not paying attention,
I'll notice my son's elbow, and wonder
how it was he ever did it.

First Grandchild Breaks the Egg with No Shell

My grandmother sent me out to get the eggs.
I was big sister now, she said; no more crying
for Mama. Too short to use the door latch,
I crawled under a canvas flap. Dark struck me
blind. Hay, yeast, feathers, sweet lime,

the air bubbled like a soup pot, a witchhouse
where iron teeth snag certain little girls
who stray too far from their mother's blessing.
From roosts on every side thrummed
a low, lazy sound, almost a growl.

I was in their territory, no mistaking it.
I knew already I'd have to lie: I couldn't reach
under the three setting hens, humming away
hidden in the dark. I patted empty nests only,
on tiptoe, the way I stretched one-handed

for pantry shelves with scissors, knives stored
out of sight. My fingers groped into an egg
and felt the yolk. I was poking the head
of a newborn, touching the back of her eyeball.
Egg white and yolk collapsed, ran down

into hushed straw. Eyes squinched closed,
I crossed the daylight to her kitchen,
carried two warm eggs with normal shells.
She heard me out, although I didn't quite
confess—I blamed it on the egg.

Because it had no shell, I said.
Because I couldn't see it. Behind my back,
my fist opening, closing, the skin
between my fingers tacky with albumin.
She knew what I'd done, but never told me

what she knew: *They need calcium,*
she announced, as if there were a remedy.
Next morning I saw our breakfast eggshells,
crushed, in a saucer in the bright chicken yard.
The hens were pecking at them,

eyeing me—standing on one foot
outside the fence—with the lidless gaze
chickens turn on the enemy.

Myopia

Horizons began to scare me
the first time we went to the delta
after I started wearing glasses.
My uncle called me *Yankee
professor,* so I went outside:

no trees, no hills, no buildings—
a plowed expanse of silt
alluvium, shuddering heat and dust,
whipped out from me in every direction.
I saw how far away the edges were.

I was a sand bur, snagged at the navel
of the flat earth—cracked groat,
in a griddlecake about to be flipped—a fly's eye,
stuck on the face of a striking clock
that whizzed through chaos like a pie pan.

I managed to lose my brand-new glasses
that afternoon, as children will do.
I'd have lost my head, too,
if it hadn't been
too late.

Four Eyes Gets Her First Warning

One day, my Mississippi uncle told me,
you gonna cross your eyes like that
and they'll stick. Said he knew
an old man'd done it once too often
—I might of seen him in town
down by the cotton gin.

The Leland boogyman.
Shuffled back and forth forever
in slit-up shoes with squash-down heels.
One eyeball pointed over
accusing the other
that leaned clear out of its socket
to point right back.

Another pastime forbidden!
and I could do high, low,
or either eye at a time.
Sole entertainment allowed
during the sermon.
Dangerous habit, he was warning—

to tinker with the flat tableau
presented me, the world
gone double at my own command:
a forest twice as many trees,
black overlapping white,
preacher and pulpit making one
voice from two mouths, and
every tongue forked.

Snake Doctor Speaks to the Apocalypse

> The dragonfly's a hundred million years older
> than the dinosaur.
> > —I say this to my mother
>
> In Mississippi, dragonfly's called snake doctor.
> > —her answer

I dream the dreams of beasts.
Lumbering ungulate bones heave
a stupid bulk around my slow slow heart.
Cow flanks shove against me, won't back off
when I try to hold ground. Firmament
of pasture grass, air warms in my nostrils,
ample tongue flops sideways in slobber.
I'm penned in the dark of the moon.
The hide on my haunches twitches
twice against the hot bite of a fly.

Now I'm the cottonmouth, slipped away
from ditches in a late May downpour
to spinecurl in sloughed magnolia leaves.
I've peeled off four legs, a second lung, eyelids.
When the ground shakes, I hear it.
It's your own resentments I work through.
I slip between the legs of your only daughter,
shove her to love, with no future.
I push steady, always forward, wind
night in the mainspring of my tail.

Tail! Dragonfly nicknames snake.
It's bright noon; she's stiff as he is supple.
Slide your meandering self this way.
I'll tell you something about survival.
You too glad to change.

You pared yourself down till now
you think you're out of sight. Listen up
to the old snake doctor. Design's what
survives. Get it right
once, then leave it alone.

You Never Get to the Horizon

In the delta, we were ringed by horizons,
the great plowed land flat as floodwater.
Cotton poisons flavored the dust
in our mouths, the air held the taste

of Egypt, after the angel passed over.
My grandmother, known
for her oyster stew: *Not many ingredients,*
she'd say and look straight at me. That look

meant *recite:* cow's milk, churned butter,
onions and salt from the commissary
on the Place, celery from the Fratisis' grocery
in town, nutmeg—hard to remember—

and last, refrain to the incantation, oysters.
Hauled upriver into our landlocked circle
from the mythical city New Orleans,
the oysters harbored the smell

of distance, wealth, corruptions of the flesh.
They were shucked in the yard by a field hand
named Calvin. Our uncle told us
Calvin killed a man with that knife.

Indoors on the stove in scalding milk, the oysters
curled like the labia of cousins who played
in the bathtub too long. My grandmother
stirred slowly, accomplished and unafraid.

At supper they'd lurk in the steaming potion
and swim unbidden into your spoon,
chewy knots, too exotic for a child's taste—
murky, like desire, remorse, even tobacco.

At some age, every granddaughter learned
to eat the oysters in her bowl. I could do it first,
the eldest. Mornings after that, if I kept out
the way, I was allowed in the kitchen

to watch Calvin pour black coffee
from cup to saucer and suck it down
with one wild slosh. He'd pretend I wasn't
there, tell the back door about Detroit,

land of promise, how he was leaving us
anyday now, his sister mail him the ticket.
Deetroit, he'd croon, looking at the ceiling—
even a little child might go, someday—

so many jobs, and houses, almost free,
how the streets there were knee-deep
with green paper money,
far as you could see.

Dry Slowly, Away from Heat

—from an old family recipe for wild rose potpourri

Spread out on paper towels, layered
with mint leaves, cloves, curls of shaved cedar,
wild rose petals fling themselves toward death

as a star can only move forward.
Each slip of bloom parches to brown veins,
Mummy's cheek, labyrinth with no plan.

When did my hand become my grandmother's,
the same fine lines, the skin? She stood me
at the window to watch the road.

Inside the sheers, the yellow air stilled,
so bright I squinted. My chin just reached the sill.
In the yard, imperious as a waiter, my uncle

dropped a thick wood match on an anthill.
The fire—silent unremarking burn—
spread long after he had walked away,

creeping down the kerosene to the throbbing queen.
Naptime, under the blanket my own hand
nudged at those private glowing places,

nubby as yesterday's ant sting.
She saw only my face. How did she know?
My bare surprised bottom reddened

under her flapping bedroom slipper. The first
smacks stirred ants crawling in new tunnels,
till pain braided its own pathways.

Late afternoon, she rushed me outside:
high-spun mullioned clouds crocheted
evenly across the sky. For a moment,

the whirling dangerous horizon sectored
firmly as clock face or dial of a compass.
Something to go by, somewhere

to stand. How long till I'm sure again?
I check the recipe. *Scent peaks just before roses
will crush into dust against your palm.*

My own kitchen, and petals spell out
her lesson remorseless as tea leaves:
somewhere silent weaving women

bind earth to sky securely
as a hole is darned in a sock.
They mind a pattern seamless as gauze,
no seam, no slub to catch the eye.

Trophy

Here is a hawk, a hunter, talons glinting,
wings spread wide, right now being nailed
to a scrap of 2 × 6. The one with the hammer,

the one even the grown-ups call uncle, goes inside
the house for a minute, to get something
he forgot. Now the others can come close.

The mouse comes first and marvels at the size.
The mouse had thought of the hawk—
her death—as swift. She learns it is huge.

A squirrel inspects an intricate trigonometry
of gray and brown feathers, the open fantail.
If the mole were here, and blessed

with a miracle, the mole alone might notice
the silent child scarcely taller than the work table
who attends these events without expression.

The hawk herself, a mechanical thinker
in the way of all birds, is puzzled
that this wide-vee cast of wings does not produce

the motion in air she expects, a landscape
sliding away beneath her. She does not see,
even with that famous eye, the one who returns

with what he needed, who picks up the board
to hang it above the garage door,
and does not bother to finish her off.

Milk Tooth

He said if I didn't poke my tongue
in the hole, the new tooth
would grow in solid gold.

He was pumping gas
and I was lolling on the floorboard,
one foot out the open car door, drowsy
in the smell of grease and old rubber,

rainbows glancing off oil spots
on the hot pavement. It was noon
and probably July and we always went
to the same filling station.

My father returned
from the tiny office, jingling change.
Much obliged, he always said
as the engine caught.

Dread and the momentum
of the old green Buick
pulling out pushed me
rolling against the back seat.

Because I'd already done it—
the porcelain wall breached,
uncornified flesh squishy,
wounded, salty—

and he'd know
as soon as he saw
the new white tooth.

Sunday Wart Charm

Fourth finger, left hand, palm side—
I bit on it when the sermon turned to redemption.
It nudged against my loosening milk teeth
the way apples elbow each other in a tilting barrel.

In Sunday school we chanted *Here is the Church,*
Here is the Steeple. When we got to *Open the Door,*
I saw the wart dangling in there, chandelier
for the sanctuary. After the service,

the grown-ups stood around the vestibule.
Hollow stumps of trapped rainwater,
a deacon's wife had heard: *frog's skin,*
a sliver moon. I'd kept my hand closed tight—

how did they know? They smiled
Baptist smiles, and the men shook hands,
stepping a half step forward. The deacon's wife
whispered, *New twig of elder, notched.*

On our way home, we swung by the Esso station.
The man who always filled our car pressed
the nozzle into my astonished hand and dripped
gas on it. The brass end of that wet gizmo

smoked vapor like a volcano.
I heard a hollow tinnitus, a sigh from
fractionated dinosaur hide and giant ferns
deep below the earth. It was the only time

he ever touched me, his fingers,
those grease-lined knuckles
I'd long admired, so hard I jumped.
Monday the wart was gone.

The church in my hands
seemed unfinished
after that. Too dark.
No way to see.

The Lens

Calvin outlived all the rest of them.
He got to be like those old people
you see in the paper, grinning
foolish above a hundred-something candles.

For a while he took to saying
he could remember things we knew
to be impossible, but then he quit claiming
he could remember anything at all.

Once I took him an old photograph
that showed me standing in front of him
in the yard behind my grandmother's kitchen.
It seemed important to let Calvin know

this busybody visitor
who brought him vanilla ice cream
was the little girl with the cowlicks
who was forever around his knees.

Sure is, he says, wadding up
his face so I see his empty gums.
That's you, I point precisely,
as I would for a toddler. He nods happily.

I move my finger, *And that's ME.*
His old blind eyes are skinned over
with light blue rheum. *Sure is,* he says
and I know he can't see a thing.

Don't you have a reading glass here?
Don't old people have these things about,
the way there's always a rattle
somewhere around a baby?

I see myself
ignore the softening ice cream
magnify the picture for him
concentrate the light

call attention to my uneven curls
silhouetted against the long, straight legs.
It's me, I shout as loud as I dare.
Sure is, he'd say, not seeing a thing.

First Grandchild Remembers a Christmas Story

Family story: when I first learned to walk
I slipped from my grandmother's house
on Christmas Eve, wobbled across the yard
in the dark, through the privet hedge
and along the gravel road.

I remember—this of course impossible—
crunching past ice skins closing in
the round edges of gritty puddles,
the cavernous shed with the tractor smell
of dried mud in the tires, crop poison.

I was somehow found
in the yard of her cook,
naked, still as wood, gazing in
through the bleared window
at a tiny, lighted tree.

The few adults in the story still alive yowl
and protest: *You weren't naked—it was winter!*
Lee Anna lived by herself, she wouldn't need a tree!
We were in town! It was the brick house next door!
And they're off on their own editions:

It was the day AFTER Christmas, couldn't get home
for Christmas Day, Daddy had to preach . . .
Mountains of presents in front of the fireplace—
you were the first grandchild, you might remember—
but you set out, hunting for more . . .

Once my aunt tried to say
it wasn't me, it was my cousin,
but she was waved down.
You had on that red velvet jacket
with white fur trim and a hood.

They never get to the practical details
you expect from adults, either—
who it was found me, how a toddler
got out of the house at all
on the longest night of the year.

My version persists, if only with me.
They want to dress me up as Santa Claus,
send me out greedy for bigger gifts,
warmer rooms, gooier sweets,
while I want to be the Christ child,

naked, and outside—drawn
to the poor icy window,
where someone else awaits,
with joy and faithful lights,
my return, my sacred birth.

Verdict

The wagon pulls up. Its iron-rimmed
oak wheels, gritty from ice melt,
split through gravel with the pop
of teeth hitting buckshot—

it couldn't have happened many times
but it always seemed to be the same:
I felt a high silent whine mount
with the late morning heat, I breathed

danger in the horses' sweat and the cold
background of salt sea, rising
from the bulging croker sack
that lay in state on melting ice.

The table for shucking oysters was set up
under the Possum oak that shaded the kitchen.
A black pot sat inside on the Chambers stove,
waiting. Company was already on its way.

I never saw my grandmother
come outside, but she was always there
in time, radiating the faint impatience
a good priest uses to propel the liturgy.

Her acolyte Calvin jimmied the first shell,
gouging at the hinge as though he had to relearn
the art. He held the open half out to her,
keeping his eyes away, outside the patch of shade.

The rudely exposed oyster swam
in a dimming nacre, the unformed palm
of an embryo—more phlegm than flesh.
She put the transparent thing in her mouth.

The sun stopped in its painful crawl
across the sky, dusty sumac leaves hung
motionless, the horses' tails did not flick.
Once I had to close my eyes.

Then she nodded
and went back inside,
the screen door shrieking open
and banging twice at her heels.

Relief leaked over us all:
the sun let out its breath, resumed
its importance and its path
down the scalded sky.

They still alive, Calvin would say
to no one in particular, ignoring
my slack face, and he and my uncle
would shake out half the sack

of heavy, wet shells
onto soft cypress boards
and commence to prise them open
with their stubby knives.

ii

Once my uncle's wife asked for her recipe.
What's your secret? was what my aunt said,
dabbing with the white dinner napkin.
My grandmother answered down the long table:
You want them to die in the hot milk.

And to know for sure, she ate the first one raw.
Ate it with the concentration of a wine merchant,
the fortunes of the chateau riding on her verdict.
No words—that quick nod, she turned,
and the afternoon relaxed and continued.

True to ceremony, when I make oyster stew
the company's already invited.
When did you shuck these oysters, Mr. Benoit?
I ask at the fish market. His answer
would be the same the day of a hurricane.

And when I make oyster stew, I know better
than to boil the milk. I give Mr. Benoit's oysters
a good sniff before I dump them in the broth.
But I shrug—the company's already on its way.
How could I tell when an oyster ceases to be alive

and begins to be dead? Only the extremes
I can understand: humming along to the music
of spheres, chock-a-block with siblings
in the shoals of the Gulf, or stinking
to high heaven the way only shellfish can.

But in between, when the shell is broached—
a mortal wound, though death's not immediate.
What did she know that I don't? her eyes glazed,
that brackish juice running along her teeth,
the purse string of her mouth pulled tight.

A shaman's journey:
trailing the soul of animal or ancestor
into realms that can't be seen
or measured with clocks or suns.

iii

Failing her nod, I suppose
we'd have hung there
around the makeshift table
by the bole of the oak tree
and slowly browned
into an old photograph
forgotten in a drawer that sticks

during winter rains. The edges
layer like a gimpy fingernail
till the picture crumbles
into fragments that make
no sense at all:

my cowlicked head
and Calvin's legs
on one piece;
another showing
my grandmother's apron,
the open gunnysack
and what's left of the ice;

on another,
half her floating hair
and her forehead
tensed in attention,
the cotton fields
stretching out behind us,
and the wagon
just about out of sight.

The horizon, a character
in its own right,
rising out of the distance
on the bright heat
outside the shade,
would skirl off
in the endless way
it always threatened to,
taking its corner
of the photograph with it.

And that would be it,
the whole show
over. No one later
would know we were

ever there or wonder
what became of us,
the drawer's contents
dumped out
when the house sold, and
the story would not go on.

But somehow the shaman
returned with a verdict,
and with her nod
the great machinery
of the afternoon
clanked to life again,
like the kitchen
in the castle
of Sleeping Beauty,

and time nudged
forward, the danger
passed, the little girl
with the uneven curls
grew up, the tree
had to be cut down,
and all the adults
in the picture
died.

iv

Whenever I let Mr. Benoit lie to me
in the fish market,
the old brown photograph
swims before my eyes.

What did she look for, so long ago,
in the salty primal liquor that swished
in her mouth and along her tongue?
the taste of life or the taste of death?

What sign should I scry? What archaic gift
was this that I failed to learn
even though I was there? And how
can she inhabit my life with such pungency

in a place she never visited without bringing
that knowledge with her? A fine crack
scrawls in the surface, spreads, the photograph
breaks apart, we are all lost.

Then, *Still alive,*
Calvin says to himself as much as to me,
interpreting the mystery yet and him dead
maybe thirty years. What wrath

would be called down if she decided .
it were not so, and upon whom?
What courage did she summon?
or which standard invoke?

We all waited for the shutter's click
while she put the raw ocean gob in her mouth,
pushed at it with her tongue,
and asked the only question there is.

Apocrypha

The river at Greenville's so wide
I could hardly see across it—
I was nearsighted

but nobody knew it yet—
brown current and whirlpools and tales
of drowned cousins and towns caving in
and high water that ate the levee
and stayed up for months.

Twice a year we returned,
steady as the equinoxes.
Coming home, they called it.
It was not home to me.

A way station in the pilgrimage:
the levee where the car touched earth again
after tightroping the long bridge from Arkansas.
My mother would suck in a deep breath

and sigh, *Now that's a river.*
She was born in this flayed dreamscape,
not four miles away, she wasn't afraid
to get out of the car, here

where the horizon shot off
in every direction, booming like cannon,
as distant—if indistinct—as the moon.
Then she'd tell us the story,

and my combative father would not disagree
which was as good as telling it himself,
how my uncle—reckless! blond!—swam
across the river the night he graduated, and

how, after he came home from the war,
he flew a crop duster under the bridge, and
for me there sprang up a giant race of ancestors
who did things we'll never be able to do again

although now my mother denies saying it
or she says it was somebody else
or that it must have been two separate men
or even that it's local legend
that couldn't possibly be true.

Watercolor Lessons

i

four girl cousins
apprenticed to a grandmother

camel-hair brushes
swept to a tip

between our lips
puckered to a little O

southern prissy tease
Kiss-me, Kiss-me-not

Mycenaean red
pursed in these lips

we mark what we kiss

ii

I never progressed   past the sunsets
    my blobs of wishwash color
        seep into each other   lose value
        go ruddy or dull

sometimes an old woman with floating hair
    hair that shines through like fine paper
        comes up behind me   thin lips
            tight to point the wet bristles

she reaches past me without pause
    without speech   one touch
        that dot   spreads on its own
            into round shoulders   egg basket
              maybe a swag of shadow

              and the paper horizon
        folds back away from me
      into distance   when I look around
    she's gone

iii

Paint rings around the light
High rag content bears
            the weight of reflection

Believe your eyes   she insists
Draw the patches of blank white light
The rest is only color

iv

            Let the tamed hands go   she whispers
Forget you know what a fence is or how
a good neighbor hammers one together

            That surface you've come to trust?
you'll see it melt   the color fail   unwilling
to countenance the heat   the dead
weight   of perspective and volume

                        Be sure to leave
some plain white paper   unparallel
unlikely   or ragged with leaf shadow
moment's wobble of earth against star
this way   only this way   only once

            The shape shift light reaches out for you
still   in the old way   when it wanted to tell you
something   before you ignored my lessons
rehearsed your eyes   to the wishes of strangers
grew up   and forgot how to see

Watercolor: Two Rockers on a Sun Porch

after a painting by Judi Betts

In the winding clockwork
of the cartwheel galaxies
                we must be reminded

all sun does not fall evenly
        even on wickerwork chairs
            so used to warming
                on morning porches.

80th Birthday, Jackson, Mississippi

sapphics for my mother

China, cheesestraws, centerpiece in fall colors.
Long distance—Me!—planning a *ladies' luncheon.*
Every call, I learn the guest list's grown shorter.
                    Mary Virginia,

Mama says. I don't even have to ask what.
You remember her—she was rich AND stingy?
Took me out to eat after church at Shoney's!
                    She'd saved some coupons.

Once last spring, she called me with two free theater
tickets: front row, center. The curtain opened.
There was sex! bad words! And we couldn't walk out
                    without being seen.

I guess it's OK to tell this—she's dead now.
Right there in our laps almost, the main actor
dropped his pants and, neither of us could help it,
                    we started giggling.

We spent intermission scrunched down in our seats,
ashamed to leave, even to use the bathroom.
With the lights back down, we laughed till we both howled
                    — two Baptist ladies!

Damn it, Mama. This story makes me jealous.
Mary Virginia found the one I needed—
mother a child wouldn't act good to hide from.
                    No. I release you—

it's enough, your friends, cousins, brothers fail. And
who am I to say you could change to please me?
Coddled ancients, ruffled and primped like schoolgirls,
          still have to die.

When it's time, though, pass up that cute, bright heaven
with the gold streets. Mary Virginia's saved seats
(senior discounts). Be glad for dark, nudge elbows.
          Laugh from the belly.

If You Transplant Parsley, Your Children Will Die

—old Cajun proverb

Under the running tap, I rinse a large bunch
of fresh parsley and there, in the wrist motion,
is my grandmother fixing supper. The Sphinx
knows, and she laughs: we crawl, walk, stump
with a cane all at once, or at least in no sequence,
across the blind face of a broken clock.

In high school biology, I heard her cackle
for the first time: *Your cells die, replace, die,
over and over. Look at your hand.* I twisted
my senior ring. *No part of it will exist seven years
from now.* I pulled silver nail polish away
in strips of moon circle—full, gibbous, quarter,

last sliver; a claw showed its dull plate
underneath. The present, the center
of a flat earth, and I am here, cooking a meal.
I turn off the water: my daughter's piano notes
toll into the kitchen. Now my own plump hand,
unlined and wearing a birthstone, practices

Ana Magdalena Bach on my grandmother's
heavy old Chickering. My other hand
shakes the wet parsley over the sink.
The metronomes on both pianos click
away, not quite in unison. Two tempi, each
necessary and unrelenting as pulse.

Fence

Say you're in kindergarten
and your teacher tells you
draw a fence. The black crayon's
thick as another thumb, you have to
bear down with your whole arm.
You mash Crayola marks
against the paper, one at a time,
and the construction paper
begins to move under your hands,
scrolling off a giant roll
she didn't tell you about. Say
you're determined to do it right
and the paper keeps coming
and you go on for a couple of years,
picket after picket, the lines
getting straighter while your fingers
thin down, and curl around the Crayola
which is now a yellow pencil
and you're scratching out
skinny rectangles, like teeth,
and you've invented
the second dimension, although
you don't call it that, and the faithful
slow-moving paper gets blue lines
like three-hole notebook sheets and
the teeth get straighter, you're taller,
have to stoop over the paper, good
drawing paper now, no blue lines,
a callus bumps up on your third finger
and your chest's getting bumpy, too,
and you look out the classroom window
at a fence and your fine muscles knit in
another dimension—the sides
of your boards crease and fold back

and a crosspiece drags its way along,
peeking between slats.

And say the teacher forgets
you in there all by yourself
with the paper and her instructions
to get it right. And you keep on
till you gaze at the fence outside
every time you look down to sketch,
and you see one of the slats
out in full sun melt like a hole
in a filmstrip and a dazzling light
sizzles out, and you look down quick
but now the slat you draw gapes
into a hole, sears open under your hands,
and a light brighter than the classroom
fluorescent you've been under so long,
brighter than the glare out the window
on the white picket fence, brighter than
anything—say those holes burn open
in the paper you're so used to and
that light underneath comes through.

BABIES' BONES FROM MAGIC CRYSTALS

Invocation

Most cooking, even of elaborate dishes, is merely the
combining of a number of very simple operations.
—*The James Beard Cookbook*

Ah, James Beard,
you died at last.
81, I read, despite
eating all that pork and mustard,
enriching the pan drippings
with heavy cream.

Step by prescribed step,
reverent as a child making mud pies,
I've rehearsed your respect for simple things:
butter melting till foam subsides;
the red flesh of healthy animals,
ground together with basil, cloves;
dough, live with yeast and winter wheat.

Inhabit my kitchen:
It's here, only here
I can believe, and not recoil.
Here, if anywhere, time stills.
We'll mix batter with our hands,
lick the spatulas, bless the bread,
whisk lead into gold, and splatter
our chests with warm sauces
till my heart bursts, too, a faithful acolyte,
from my own 80 years of ravishing appetite.

Written While Baking Easter Dragons

I'm up early to make Easter dragons
from a friend's recipe—a traditional spring bread,
she told me, from the island of Crete. Made with yeast,
flour, butter, honey, hot milk, salt. Shaped
into a cheerful beast with four skink feet, a tail,
goggly eyes, a red boiled egg poking out of its mouth.

I've had the taste of honey and warm milk in my mouth
since before daylight. The first step in the dragon
recipe calls for a milk broth, one you'd imagine in a tale
about lost children, what they'd sop dry bread
in, fattened up by crones in the deep woods—old women shaped
into witches by loneliness. The yeast

goes in next, one package, quick-rising yeast
you soften in water. I tested the broth against my mouth
for temperature. Can't be too hot, or the bread has no shape.
Sucked my fingers. It was still dark. There's a dragon
coming and I suck sweet lukewarm milk, a child crumbling bread
to leave as markers on the path: the fairy tale

reminds me I don't know the story of this Cretan beast, its tail
growing in my kitchen, its scales cut by my scissors, its yeasty
breath flowing hot around an egg. A bread
monster I invite here unknowing, its mouth
yawning wide now in the oven, its fearful dragon
eyes, claws pressed in with fork tines, reptile shape.

How did I know what shape
to mash its feet? which way to curl its tail?
Is it female or male? What order of dragon
rises on yeast
and sweet butter? What mouth
opens at dawn with the smell of bread?

How much fear is baked into plain bread?
How dangerous the slow gluten swell of dough? what shape
might it carry into our innocent mouths,
doubling on its own, slower than a clock hand? No tailor-
made answers come, just the silent ferment of yeast
and steady kitchen heat like the breath of a dragon.

Day. The Easter dragon is brown, ready to eat, its breadcrust
skin amber with egg glaze, the yeast's work done. Salamander shape,
earth spirit tail. Take. Eat. Power of the dark, in our mouths.

Denmother's Conversation

Denmother went to college in the 60s,
could pin your ears back at a cocktail party.
Her laugh had an edge to it,
and her yard was always cut.

She grew twisted herbs in the flower beds,
hid them like weeds among dumpy marigolds.
The wolfsbane killed the pansies
before they bloomed much.

She'd look at you real straight and talk
about nuclear power plants or abortion. At home
alone she boiled red potatoes all night
to make the primitive starch that holds up the clouds.

Hostess

She sliced all the green grapes in half
and laid them in a circle, cut side down,
around the edge of the wheel of ripe brie.

Then she stuck a toothpick
in the center of the wheel
with the last whole grape
on it, like a flag.

It was a sign she had gone mad,
you see. But nobody noticed.
The guests ate all the brie and all the grapes
and licked their lips again and again.

They made little wads of their napkins
and dropped them on the table,
and then they went home.

Denmother's Vacation

Denmother mowed her lawn close,
locked bikes in the garage closet.
Her porch light burned pale in the daytime
and neighborhood dogs roamed freely about.

The mailman skipped her box for days.
Wet birch leaves stuck to the sidewalk.
At last, lights are seen again inside her house.
The moon wanes, the equinox is past.

She digs in her flower beds, late afternoons,
mulches the new plants with kitchen compost.
Not far down the block, a big yellow dog
gets run over by a truck delivering packages.

Rainbow Room

I was twenty-four, pregnant,
cartoon neck-crane tourist
in skyscraper city. We *drove* there
from Baton Rouge—didn't know
you don't take a car to Manhattan.
One of those blissful pregnancies

where every time I sat down
I'd go to sleep. Went to sleep
during a tour of the UN,
we were asked to leave for loitering.
Our big splurge: the Rainbow Room,
RCA Building. My first elevator

to 77 stories. It was 1968,
you know how you time things
by your children. *Duke Ellington at the Keys*,
the standup signboard in the lobby said,
and we added in, when we got to the glass doors,
two or three guys playing nameless back-up.

No more than ten feet from the piano,
I put my elbow on the table,
propped my head, and sank back
into that golden estrogen gestation nap
I roused from only when I was moving.
That's my excuse for missing the Great One,

but in truth I've never been too good
at taking in what happens in the present.
My husband still tells this story at parties
now and then, making people laugh when
I sleep through two whole sets. I don't feel
too bad about it anymore. I do remember

the 360 horizon of city lights
from the highest windows I'd ever visited,
and besides, it was chilly outside
and warm in there where
the little tadpole—beyond category—
didn't have a gender or a name. A new sound

twinkled into her round round universe,
muffled a little bit on the high notes. She's not
one to miss a thing. Her tiny ears unfurled.
Right away, she started wanting to come out—
ready or not—come out
where all that close harmony was.

Warning

His hair is light as dandelion fluff
and wanders with the air as if to float
away. The sun streaks bars across his throat
and cheek that bind my heart. Experts rebuff
me for this: a mother ought not to pleasure
herself quite this way—a lapse of duty—
too much like lover's eyes, pride of beauty,
senses gloating on ill-gotten treasure.
But this one came to me with so much grace,
such prowess in his limbs, a puppy's eyes,
he floods me through with Queen Jocasta's joy
and I am helpless gazing on his face.
Let old men, Freud to Moses, criticize:
I alone am mother of this boy.

My Dreams Last Night Were Thick with Salt

—over coffee at Navarre Beach

my sheets had fallen in the surf
and line-dried stiff in the Gulf breeze.

My children rubbed at rinds of salt
around their eyes, the dog licked ashy lines
from their brown legs. Water from the hose
tastes funky, they whined.

Is it tears you dream? Salt
for the dead? The thumping brine
we haul about as sloshing, ruminating
two-legged bags of mother estuary?

Stagnant smell of the trapped
sea water and soggy towels—
grass burned yellow in patches,
all the leaves drop from the tomatoes.

Maybe you dream the stuff itself
as a chemist would see it,
shifting in form only, not substance,
from ion to crystal and back to ion,
the compound in sweat that stings a sunburn
the same as the snowflake crust at tidemark?

Coffee mugs—left out by wicker chairs—
grow bristly rims of salt inside. Fish scales
bunch glittery on the cypress rail.

Maybe you dream you're Lot's wife,
looking back at what you leave behind
instead of forward to a house without memory.

Glazing thin to rhinestone grit,
urine splash from the hound next door
marks the bottom banister.

Why did she turn, against the weight
of those bad-natured old gods?

A fishhook, gouged in the wood decking,
waves a snip of leader sharp as whiskers.

Regret for a sooty cast-iron skillet
that made nice pancakes? Or for the stool
she left behind that was her mother's? Maybe
she lagged to shoo a dawdling toddler.

Behind me, calling me,
the sun smokes red through brackish haze.

Who's to say she mourned the fleshpots
or sodomy or god-knows-what unspeakable sins?
What's the worst thing it could be?

I turn to look: the blood-surge in my heart
collapses—a handful of silvery powder.
My gaze dries over like clouding fish eyes,
the sway in my breasts as I turn, sets . . .

Denmother Lists Her House with a Realtor

Denmother lived in suburbia,
had nothing whatever to do
with scouts. She bought a red brick
ranch-style and inside it she grew
babies' bones from magic crystals.

She shopped at the A&P, after noon,
often wore a tennis dress.
The babies' bones grew apace—
she traded for a Toyota wagon.

The bones filled the house, finally,
clear to the ceilings—
den, 3 bedroom, 2½ bath.
When they spilled over into the carport,
Denmother left the neighborhood.

Denmother Volunteers at the School Carnival

Denmother told fortunes at the Halloween carnival
in a little tent the PTA fixed up for her booth.
The carnival chairman found a crystal ball somewhere,
stuck a flashlight in it wrapped in tissue paper.

She wore gypsy hoops, and boots, and a black wig.
A Pirate cried when he saw her eye make-up.
The children in line said she'd gaze in the ball
and say your boyfriend's name or your favorite color.

The corners on Superman's breastplate curled
and the bulb in the flashlight dimmed to orange.
The Princesses began to look seedy, ate too much candy.
Denmother read palms, then. Said when they would die.

Bone Fires

I light candles to begin the Seder,
striking the match self-consciously
across a red paper matchbook,
the printed advertisement out of place
with the linen and rubbed silver.

A sacrilege, probably: the shiksa mother,
who hears all music as variations
on sturdy Protestant hymns in 4/4 time,
singing plangent baruchas by rote
in a generic foreign accent
assumed years ago in French class.

The candles, kindling to the match,
shine back at me from my children's eyes.
The archaic modes of the baruchas
curl around the flickering reflections,
and their eyes are alien to me
as cats' eyes, old as Egypt.

Shaking out the match, I see my hand
freckled, Protestant, sunburned dry
from a long day in the open. The puff
of sudden smoke off the dead match rises
from evening fires of cypress driftwood,
silent on the levee in the Mississippi delta.

The Dress

The dress I wore in the dream:
white batiste, embroidered
with patient eyelet stitches.
Fitted bodice, sashed waist, gathered long skirt.
The sleeves puffed full from narrow shoulders
and pulled in above the elbow.

A wedding dress and a nightgown
at the same time: at once
too seductive and too childish.
Never thought of changing into something else.
Felt uncomfortable the whole time.

In this dress, I lounged in amber lamplight
with a lover from college. He played tunes for me
on a broken ukulele. Made me smile,
and wonder what my husband thought.

I left the room and, outside,
rescued a baby falling from his stroller.
I played with him happily at a family reunion.
He'd been forgotten by his mother.
I left him to someone else.

Then I walked barefoot past great, sighing machines
with huge tires, working steady, laying a street.
An asphalt spreader oozed thick, steaming surface.
The melted oil splattered my skirt in sticky chunks.

I went inside again
and faced the mirror:
my breasts showed clearly
through the thin fabric of the dress.

Galapagos in the Felicianas

East Feliciana Parish, Louisiana

The weeds here have their own names,
ratcheted into alphabet and phyla
snug as Paul Scarlet roses:

dock, goat's-rue, pyracantha,
loosestrife, kudzu on the spalling bluffs,
heal-all (the *Prunella vulgaris*), Christ crown;

summoned by the *traiteuse* who learned leaves
from Chitimacha for love charms, blood-stanch,
the lazy eye; jerked backhanded from okra mulch

by a sunburned farmwife who reaches
across crooked woman-chopped rows
to pinch a ballooning caterpillar

off her tomatoes; dubbed into Latin
by taxonomists with binomial leanings
who came from somewhere else.

Even so, these loblolly hills—isolate as Petri plates—
foster other green offspring that have no names,
that slip between the knees of lost daughters,

before daylight when air holds anarchy—
hawk's cry, shrike, whatever eats the cheerful
tree frog, the gristly creak of hurrying possum—

an hour before Catahoulas bay or pickups
scrabble gravel roads unmarked on maps:
leaves with two stems. Freshwater shreds

that twist in eel shapes, beneath sumac
reflecting black in standing ponds,
and never emerge. Flagellates

with uncounted heads. And parasites,
old as fern spores, that root
in the forest of fur or hair
of no known color.

Love's Complexion

I've given him an imperfect mantle,
this son, thirteen years old. A scatter of lights
scrawls his cheeks, constellations

whirling the night sky.
Each new Orion waxes and wanes
in sync with the moon.

Noxema, Clearasil
smell seeps under the door. I conjure up
witch hazel, arsenic—

Hot water,
I want to command. *Soap. And
keep your hands off.*

But the lab door's shut,
the retort stoppered and boiling.
The ear of the adept leans

not toward his mother—failed
old hag-woman in her chocolate house—
toward science, toward hope.

Shopping

for Carroll

She's 14. Alternates from sybarite
to saint. All school week, her hair's been curly.
Sunday, she blow-dries it straight. *Where's Shirley
Temple?* Wrong note! I blunder on: *Your . . .* Spite
curdles her voice: *You're just like a MOTHER.*
Hours at the mall with her girlfriends. She tries
on outfit after outfit—she's my size
now—cameo roles, any costume other
than herself or me. At childhood's boundary,
who is she? Who am I at middle age?
She hates my words; I taught her to speak.
We're both experimenting, our quandary
the same. My job is guru, woman, sage
example; hers, to find what I seek.

Coelenterata: Navarre Beach

The early morning sea is brown,
the shore littered with stranded jellyfish.
My eyes are swollen from yesterday's salt,
the margaritas, a smoky Holiday Inn pillow.
One scrap of last night's dream bobs free,
summoned by the festering ocean:
     my own head, sundered
          from its neck.

The water is full of these things!
a whine, our first words of the morning.
We've carried coffee to the beach, in styrofoam,
to wake up easy by a tourist ocean. But before
it tips, each breaker thins to show us
red-tentacled tissue against the trough behind—
     ugly clots, slack, without will, pulsed
          only by the single-minded surf.

No brain, my factual daughter recalls:
No skeleton. 99 percent water. They are nothing but sacks.
And then an adolescent gearshift from scientist
to theologian: *So how do they die?* The viscous blobs
evaporate to nothing as the sand heats up.
How do they live? my only answer at middle age.
My bloated dream unsnags its drowned moorings,
buoys toward me out of sleep:
     severed head, eyes open,
          passed from hand to hand.

Sighting

I plan to stare at the horizon all day,
to relax my neck, let go my old griefs.
But the sloshing surf drags down my eyes,
provokes a squawl of gulls, undermines
the castles of loudmouth boys. Sand and sunscreen
crawl in my sweaty suit. And lovers promenade,
rubbed over every tanned inch with coconut oil or Panama Jack,
the huge sea behind them soup stock of their own desire.

I try again. My eyes, lifted into the glare,
sting from last night's piña coladas, salt swim.
The planet rim I have in mind smudges in a Gulf haze.
I squint for distance: the farthest waves draw my eyes,
running off the world curve in a shudder. I see
whale bodies roll over, impossible in scale that far off.
Then the earth leans away to India or China,
becomes a map, and I have lost my place again.

There is no line, I cannot fix it.
No rubicon where ions, having enough of sea
or filling enough with sun, leap for and become sky.
These rowdy sand engineers must draw it when they go
home to school: beach and ocean a double stripe—
yellow, green Crayola on construction paper.
Sky, a layer of stiff blue wax, rubbed hard
across the very top of the page.

Down the strand, three brown pelicans pop into flight,
straight off threatened species' lists, homilies for Mother's Day.
Sure enough, there are the unselfish gabble throats,
the martyred breasts, swollen feet from Audubon prints.
They wingbeat low in a tight unison, all dull feather
and hollow bone creaking above children in bright lycra,
trace the water's hissing edge—with unpredicted grace—
and finally out of sight.

Waiting: A Family *I Ching*

WHAT I AM

Here is what I am. I'm a sleeping dog with loose skin. An old bottle made of thick glass, with candle tallow. Among the kinds of soil, I am the chalky. A crack in the floor through which serpents can enter. Among serpents, the thick black ones. A black snake that suns herself on fallen cypress. Flesh of a papaya. A light sunburn.

WHAT HE IS

Myopia. Hoarseness. Hunting dogs with heavy shoulders. Among the kinds of soil, a sandy loam. In mountains, low cliffs of red sandstone. Among the kinds of dreams, those of cars and driving at night at high speeds. The currents of warm rivers. Anger held in the throat. Whiskey. Cloves. Of trees, the young sycamores. Boats of all kinds. Boats being launched. Boats being moored.

ELDEST DAUGHTER

Books of maps. The lowest voices. Small fingers. Animals, always brown. Sandals. Sport of all seasons. Of the kinds of soil, alluvium. Sleep. Long-haired cats of no lineage. Indigo-blue dye, in silk or linen. Low waterfalls with no foam. The deep rock-scour beneath waterfalls. A roof of gray shingles with a leak that damages nothing.

SON

Shoulders. Numbers. Dreams of thieves. Fast-growing leafy plants. Steel weapons, well oiled. Gunpowder. Of harmonies, the ones with chords and open sixths. Bags made of string. Red meat. The weather. In oceans, the deep upwellings of cold. Fish with large scales. Speed. Diseases with high fever and little pain. Clear hot sky with clouds only in the evening.

ANGER

Vermilion. Whiskey. A hawk. A damp warm afternoon moving in over a clear morning. It is a muddy slow river. It is tarry sludge from chemical plants. Phosphorus. Styrofoam that snags at high water on the levee. In the night sky, it is not Mars but Antares. Eldest daughter in a family with no sons. All reed instruments. A broken pottery bowl in the gravel of the driveway. The bones of the hand.

ANGER IN THE THROAT

A hemp rope. The root of a mast, pulling against wind. Boils, not yet come to the surface. Crust of trash at the edge of an oxbow. A highway tunnel under a bay. The danger of chemical fires. It is things caught between. The dream of a dead-end alley, sided by tall buildings. Mother and baby who live on the street. Baby whose neck is soft as rotten celery. A dream you go back to for years. It is fish. Fish that feed in mud and filth. Catfish. Choupic. Gar.

RESENTMENT

Lemon-grass tea. Teeth that need brushing. The color chartreuse. Fear of walking too far. A candle wick that plays out halfway. Broken cuticles. Of dreams, those of being dragged behind a wagon. Urine released into brown pine needles. Car door that won't open. In the sky, a rain that will not fall. Underground, magnesium, the phosphates, copper oxide. Deep mines that are not productive, where lives are lost. Outside the mine shaft, slag.

Family Vacation, Complete with Whiplash

England, out of Warwickshire. North Atlantic sun. What Robin Hood
drove this way before? I'm shotgun, rented car, two-lane road,
and a hand-lettered sign speeds by on our left—remember,
we're driving on the wrong side—*Fresh berries. Pick
your own Gooseberries/Raspberries/Dewberries.* He brakes
—O Jack! three beans for your cow!—jerks right to U-turn

through an island, around another sign, *No turns,*
right again, and bulging up behind us, the grill & hood
of a Toyota jeep, wide steel bumper, squalling brakes—
just topped a rise off the Motorway onto this shire road,
we find out later—the sound a miner's pick
cracking into anthracite's what I remember

and a BOCK, for an echo. Seconds I don't remember
at all. The pop had replied from my own neck, when it turned
a way it wasn't meant to go, as if a human head could pick
its vista, cant to any vantage, face unhooded
eyes toward any sight—consecrate or unholy—ride
manshod over symptoms, deny it's falling down that breaks

your crown, that tendons strip, porches have edges, eggs broken
to make omelets cannot be put together again, misremembering
all the king's horses and all the king's men riding
those horses. Holiday UK had taken a fresh turn!
I'd looked at something I shouldn't! Now Red Riding Hood
couldn't pretend she never left the oak-shade path to pick

wildflowers, couldn't pretend she didn't hand-pick
the blue lupine she knew would break
her mother's heart and sully the red hood
and cape, that she just couldn't remember
the simple turns
in the acorn-crunchy road

that led to Grandmother's. I came to. The tar macadam road
surface around our car spangled with broken glass. I picked
shards out of my hair, still dizzy, turned
them over and over, tiny crystal balls in the white sun. And broke
from the past. I can scarcely remember
the woman driven south toward Warwickshire that day, who'd

hoodwinked herself into taking the well-marked road
stretching out of fairy tale into memory. Or why she picked
that odd moment to make the break. Right after the raspberry fields.
       Right after the U-turn.

You Better Enjoy This, It's Costing a Fortune

—overheard in a lift line

This is not my sport,
skiing. I'm missing
the urge to conquer
a mountain, master
the oldest fear, falling.
Some Celtish goodwyf
ancestor, ankles thick
with pregnancy and potato
winters, straightens up
from smearing pitch
on the ewe's hoof, stretches
with her hand to the small of her back,
and laughs.

A raven eases by overhead
and I'm freed from the round of play
—conveyor up, slide down,
conveyor up again—
unsnap my boot bales and rub
the dent in my pasty shins.
I sit to face the other
peaks. They laugh, too,
at this resort slope
that's shaved
for runs, groomed nightly,
powdered by snow cat,
spangled with tourists
bright as popsicles, in Gortex,
Ecco goggles, knit
caps with matching
pompoms. The pompoms
schuss sine curves
down and down and down.

With my teeth, I drag off
gloves lined with Thinsulate.
The goodwyf laughs again, gone
inside now, sitting down
to nurse the twins.
She wishes me well,
does not wish she were here.
Look out my eyes, I say.
I brought you here.

At the ski rental, boots
in my shoe size refused
to close around my calves.
Nordic models on wall posters
flashed their large even teeth.
I confessed to the clerk,
a beautiful Teuton:
my small feet, short heavy legs.
*No boots
made for that,* his expression tics.
Shit jobs in paradise,
my face twists in return.

In Condo AmeriKhan
my teen-age son has suffered
possession by a Tartar grandfather
from the most forbidden steppes.
He flings himself on the couch.
Bring me water,
he growls, a stranger.
Want that with mare's blood?
his father parries.
The boy speaks
a marauder's language
we can't understand:
vamps moguls on Devil's Crotch,
Spinal Tap; tucks Jack Ripper,
checks out the double blacks.

The macho forebear
may be a Viking—the boy's
boots fit perfectly.

It snows rarely in Somerset,
says the goodwyf, untying her dress front
with puffy wintersore fingers.
A wet cold, overcast for months.
Lambs' feet rot, the childer
itch chilblains. Colorado sun
fuses the pompoms
to colored glass. Marbles
roll out the lift top
in handfuls, head down.
I dose with 16 Eclipse.
A new fever blister bumps up
under the PreSun lip block.
I get along, she says.

But look across, I say
to her. *This is the new land,*
the Arapaho Peaks, the Great Divide.
Bearing apron pockets of tundra
and snow fields, upthrust granite
notches into sherd puzzle;
the high-altitude sky curls
into a bowl with broken rim.
Earth crust and turquoise dome
fit together snug,
the inside of an eggshell.

And there, below timberline,
I say. Boreal forests
that survived an ice age
trend the high ranges southward.
From this distance,
the woods lose spruce,
juniper, lodgepole pine,

smudge to a painter's
single black/blue ground.
We are too high for meadows.
Look, I say to her again.
I bring you here.

Her milk has let down.
I look out for her,
and she smiles.

Waiting for Dark

Eve of All Hallows, two days shy of the Day of the Dead.
Feast of pumpkins. Pagan Samhain. Already, where the crape myrtle
twists out of the ground rising like smoke, thin shadows
see their chance, streak across the low grass. All souls walk
tonight. They slip from the cleft between seasons. Unless we appease
them, they addle daughters, crack the cat's milk bowl, suck the tender

genitals of our sons. I offer chestnuts, a pomegranate, tender
ripe persimmons, a seed plume of wild sedge—abracadabra the dead
to come to me, drawn by this candle, appeased
in their smoke-filled brainpans by my gifts. The crape myrtle
stretches higher, pale bole smooth as the legs of boys walking
jostly against each other, whistling in the shadows.

Where bole leaves root, the ground slit's muscled wider. More shadows
race out. The veil between worlds is thin. Light grows tender
as the afternoon drains slowly out of the leaves. Soon the sidewalk
will writhe ghosts, witches with plastic bags, black masks with dead-
white skulls, Wal-Mart pirates, styrofoam pumpkins thumping the myrtle
branches, princesses in pink rouge who hope to appease

the Dark Queen when their own mothers won't call her name. Appease
me tonight—you who left me, deserted me for the company of shadows!—
I warm pennies for your lids, bind my forehead with myrtle,
stack oak logs in threes, shave cedar for fragrant tinder,
carve jacklantern eyes to spy embers riding dead
sockets, the red stare of visitors who walk

tonight only. Now, I look out pumpkin eyes, a flame walks
back and forth under my scalp, smears oily soot. Appease
my hollow sorrow—I'm straked of pulp, of seeds, a dead
mouth with ragged orange teeth, breath of shadows
from the slumping candle, damp walls, tender
scorched flesh, smell of burnt feathers, wax, myrrh. Till

you come back to me I'm bound in this vigil. Till the myrtle
grove on your grave shudders like young limbs in love, till you walk
forth, find your way to me, reach chilly fingers to my tender
gourd-flesh gums, sagging eye holes, till you appease
the woman of shadows
who sliced my face and left me for dead.

The candle goes dead, fills me with smoke. I hear the rattle of myrtle
seeds, taste the blood of pomegranates—join ground shadows to walk
across the last light, fever appeased, scars no longer tender.

Carving Jack

The knife
is not so sharp this year,
the plunge less desperate
into the awkward orange head. I went too late
to the grocery, after the good pumpkins
were gone. The children are grown.
The doorbell rings a few times
in an empty house.

The long blade jams at the hilt,
violent and impotent as an ax
seized in the dying clamp of green wood.
Caught in the act, I manage
a lopsided breath and remember the wobble
— every year reinvented—
dentist luxating a molar
before the slickened withdrawal.

Now my deep competent slices slow-walk
pigeon-toed around the stem, the earthbinding
comes unplugged. Always the surprising depth
of ocher flesh beneath the rind, and
damp vegetable air
inside, stupid with waiting.

One can't do things perfectly
in the stringy cavity. The seeds should be
saved for spring, or washed and toasted.
Webby entrails tangle my fingers, gum
my reaching arm. The dark bowl is
round/wet/physical as the hollow of a uterus.
You are mine now, my clammy beauty—stripped
from the sine curve of offspring/ancestor

by the laser of my attention. The mouth
pulls out in three sections—evil intention,
guilty confusion, idiot grin. One cheek
spore-pocked, mildewed. This is the produce
no one would buy. It won't stand
upright on its own. I see it failing
in the patch, lumpen among velcro leaves.

A left eye slides open. A spiky eyebrow.
The face changes its mind with every feature.
The dead will not walk to this lantern,
this year. Let them stay dead for once—
old men who clutch their cheesy secrets,
the two babies, so many women gone blind.
All seeds cannot grow, there is not
room enough on this battered earth.
I slough the sticky mess into the ivy,
think, Let the wasps come.

The doorbell again. There are no children
I can recognize under the old sheets
and KMart witch hats.
Ah! Lean the awful thing
against the brick steps
and light the candle.
                    I am done with it.

Mrs. Calendar Negotiates the Xmas Rush

Mrs. Calendar, overworked and slightly resentful
even during simpler months, was surprised
by an occasional small pleasure in December.
The sudden taste of cloves or ginger
could pierce her list-quick efficiency,
not with peace, to be sure, but at least
with pure sensation. Already, balsam candles
in a chilly house had made her pause a half step
when she came in the back door with the groceries.

But the story of the baby kept her uneasy.
Mrs. Calendar acknowledged chance, of course—
her policy: to allow a certain margin
for luck, good or bad—but this went too far.
The unplanned child, born at solstice
when dark and cold reach their bound,
stared accusingly at Mrs. Calendar
from every second Christmas card.
Now, of all times, when she had so much
to do, the story confounded her: the warmth
and hope that had not been scheduled,
the light from unexpected sources.

Acknowledgments

The author expresses deep gratitude to the editors of the following publications for publishing the poems listed and for their invaluable advice and support: *Anemone*, "First Grandchild Breaks the Egg with No Shell" (1986); *Apalachee Quarterly*, "Denmother's Conversation" (1989); *Asylum*, "Denmother Volunteers at the School Carnival" under a slightly different title (1990); *Birmingham Poetry Review*, "Waiting: A Family *I Ching*" (2003); *Bogg*, "Warning" (1988); *California Quarterly*, "Bone Fires" (1987); *Cimarron*, "Conjugal Love Poem" (2004); *Exquisite Corpse*, "Rainbow Room" (www.corpse .org, No. 11); *Hudson Review*, "Verdict" (1988); *Louisiana Cultural Vistas*, "Choosing Monogamy" in a slightly different version (Vol. 8, No. 4); *Louisiana English Journal*, "Envoi: Billy Doo" under the title "Valentine Letter" (n.s., Vol. 7, No. 1); *Louisiana Literature*, "All the Men in My Family Hunt" (1999), "Old Grandmother Magic" (1990); *Mildred*, "Written While Baking Easter Dragons," "*You Better Enjoy This, It's Costing a Fortune*" (both Vol. 4, No. 1); *Nebraska Review*, "Milk Tooth," "Rare Night Out" under the title "One of Those Movies" (both 1988); *Northwest Review*, "Fence" (Vol. 29, No. 1), "Sighting" (Vol. 25, No. 2), "Heat," "What the Magnolias Say" (both Vol. 26, No. 2); *open 24 hrs*, a portion of "Watercolor Lessons" under a slightly different title (No. 10); *Poet Lore*, "First Grandchild Remembers a Christmas Story" (1987); *Poetry Motel*, "Hostess" (1985); *Potato Eyes*, "Hunting and Gathering" under the title "Love Poem" (1993); *Primavera*, "Waiting for Dark" (1995); *Slant*, "Mrs. Calendar Negotiates the Xmas Rush" (2004); *The Sun*, "Aphrodite" (1999); *Taos Review*, "Four Eyes Gets Her First Warning," "Snake Doctor Speaks to the Apocalypse" (both 1990); *Visions International*, a portion of "Watercolor Lessons" under the title "White Picket Fence"; *Wind*, "Quarrel: An Aftermath" (2003); *Zone 3*, "The Dress," "Sunday Wart Charm" (both

1988), "You Can See It in the Architecture" (1991). "Invocation" first appeared in *The Hungry Poet's Cookbook* (Long Beach, CA: Applezaba Press, 1987), ed. Glenda McManus. "White House in Watercolor" first appeared in *Louisiana Laurels* (Baton Rouge: Arts Council of Greater Baton Rouge, 1992), ed. Donald Stanford.

The following poems first appeared in the chapbook *Built in Fear of Heat*, published by Nightshade Press in 1994: "Apocrypha," "*Dry Slowly, Away from Heat,*" "Galapagos in the Felicianas," "*If You Transplant Parsley, Your Children Will Die,*" "Myopia," "The Lens," "You Never Get to the Horizon." The following poems first appeared in the chapbook *Kitchen Heat*, published by Maude's Head Press in 1991: "Denmother Lists Her House with a Realtor," "Denmother's Vacation," "*My Dreams Last Night Were Thick with Salt,*" and "Love's Complexion."